CN00686947

FOUR WINDS

POEMS FROM INDIAN RITUALS

Gene Meany Hodge

Sunstone Press
Santa Fe, New Mexico

DEDICATION

To the Indians of the Southwest
whose beauty of thought and expression,
and unity with nature and all living
things are an inspiration.

G.M.H.

Illustrations of Father Sky and Mother Earth
from a silk screen print of the sandpainting,
courtesy of the Wheelwright Museum, Santa Fe, New Mexico

Drawings— Gene Meany Hodge

Copyright © 1977 by Gene Meany Hodge. All Rights Reserved.

No part of this book may be reproduced in any form or by any electronic
or mechanical means including information storage and retrieval systems,
without permission in writing from the publisher, except by a reviewer
who may quote brief passages in a review.

Printed in the United States of America

10   9   8   7   6   5   4

Library of Congress Cataloging in Publication Data:

Hodge, Gene Meany, comp.
    Four Winds.
    Bibliography: p.
    1. Indian poetry — Translation into English
    2. American poetry — Translations from Indian languages.
I. Title
PM 198.E3H59   1977   897   77-17800
ISBN: 0-913270-07-5

Published by   SUNSTONE PRESS
                Post Office Bos 2321
                Santa Fe, NM 87504-2321 / USA
                (505) 988-4418 *orders only* (800) 243-5644
                FAX (505) 988-1025

INTRODUCTION

While doing research for my book, *THE KACHINAS ARE COMING, Pueblo Indian Kachina Dolls With Related Folktales*, I found so much beauty and poetry in the Indian philosophy that I have selected a few poems for a small book. The illustrations are symbolic Indian designs which I have made into compositions to fit the poems and prayers.

I am grateful to all the students of Indian ceremonial life who have made it possible for us to know the beautiful philosophy and religion of the Indians. The material for this book is gathered from these early works. Many of these prayer-poems are free translations from long nine-day ceremonies, some for rain and abundant harvests, some for healing, some for blessing, and some for thanksgiving.

The writer also wishes to express her appreciation for courtesies extended by the staff of The Museum of Navaho Ceremonial Art, Santa Fe, New Mexico, to the librarian, Mrs. Mary Bryan of the Library of The Museum of New Mexico at The Laboratory of Anthropology, Santa Fe, New Mexico, and to all the friends who encouraged me.

Gene Meany Hodge

BIRD AMONG FLOWERS AND RAINBOW

THE VOICE THAT BEAUTIFIES THE LAND

The voice that beautifies the land!
The voice above,
The voice of the thunder
Within the dark cloud
Again and again it sounds,
The voice that beautifies the land.

The voice that beautifies the land!
The voice below;
The voice of the grasshopper
Among the plants
Again and again it sounds,
The voice that beautifies the land.

From the Navaho Mountain Chant
translated by Dr. Washington Matthews

THE HAKO, A PAWNEE CEREMONY

Oh Morning Star, for thee we watch!
Dimly comes thy light from distant skies;
We see thee, then lost art thou.
Morning Star, thou bringest life to us.

Oh Morning Star, thy form we see!
Clad in shining garments dost thou come,
Thy plume touched with rosy light.
Morning Star, thou now art vanishing.

Oh youthful Dawn, for thee we watch!
Dimly comes thy light from distant skies;
We see thee, then lost art thou.
Youthful Dawn, thou bringest life to us.

Oh youthful Dawn, we see thee come!
Brighter grows thy glowing light
As near, nearer thou dost come.
Youthful Dawn, thou now art vanishing.

Day is here! Day is here, is here!
Arise my son, lift thine eyes. Day is here! Day is here, is here!
Look up my son, and see the day. Day is here! Day is here, is here
Day is here! Day is here, is here.

translated by Alice Fletcher

MORNING STAR KACHINA

SONG TO THE PLEIADES

Look as they rise, up rise
Over the line where sky meets the earth;
Pleiades!
Lo! They ascending, come to guide us,
Leading us safely, keeping us one;
Pleiades.
Teach us to be, like you, united.

From THE HAKO, A PAWNEE CEREMONY
translated by Alice Fletcher

WHEN THE TEWA CHILD IS NAMED

The mother and godmother on the housetop
before dawn. The godmother speaks:

My Sun! My Morning Star!
Help this child to become a man.
I name him
Rain-dew Falling!
I name him
Star Mountain!

The mother throws a live coal. The godmother
throws sacred cornmeal.

From SONGS OF THE TEWA
translated by Dr. Herbert Joseph Spinden

SUN FATHER

Who among men and the creatures
Could live without the Sun Father?
For his light brings day, warms and gladdens the
Earth Mother with rain which
Flows forth in the water we drink
And that causes the flesh of the
Earth Mother to yield seeds abundantly.

Philosophy of a Zuni Sun Priest
ZUNI BREADSTUFF
by Frank Hamilton Cushing

A PRAYER ON THE ADOPTION OF A FRIEND

My child! This day I take you in my arms and clasp
       you strongly,
And if it be well, then our father the sun will, in
       his road over the world, rise, reach his zenith,
Hold himself firmly, and smile upon you and me that
       our roads of life may be finished.
Hence I grasp you by the hand with the hands and hearts
       of the gods. I add to thy wind of life
That our roads of life may be finished together.
My child, may the light of the gods meet you! My child,
       Thil-a-wa.

One of the Zuni Elders taken to Washington
and Boston in 1882 by Frank Hamilton Cushing,
became so fond of one of Cushing's friends that
he formally adopted him.
From MY ADVENTURES IN ZUNI
by Frank Hamilton Cushing

A BLESSING

*May the Great Spirit send his
    choicest gifts to you;
May the Sun Father and the Moon Mother
    shed their softest beams on you;
May the Four Winds of Heaven
    blow gently upon you and
Upon those with whom you share
    your heart and home.*

                           *Attributed to the
                           Coahuila Indians*

SUN KACHINA

PRAYER OF A PAWNEE INDIAN SHAMAN

I know not if the voice of man can reach to the sky;
I know not if the Mighty One will hear as I pray;
I know not if the gifts I ask will all be granted;
I know not if the word of old we truly can hear;
I know not what will come to pass in our future days;
I hope that only good will come, my children, to you.

I now know that the voice of man can reach to the sky;
I now know that the Mighty One has heard as I prayed;
I now know that the gifts I asked have all been granted;
I now know that the word of old we truly have heard;
I now know that Tirawa harkens unto man's prayer;
I know that only good has come, my children, to you.

From THE HAKO, A PAWNEE CEREMONY
translated by Alice Fletcher

SONG OF THE SKY LOOM

Oh our Mother the Earth, oh our Father the Sky,
Your children are we, and with tired backs
We bring you the gifts that you love.
Then weave for us a garment of brightness;
May the warp be the white light of morning,
May the weft be the red light of evening,
May the fringes be the falling rain,
May the border be the standing rainbow.
Thus weave for us a garment of brightness
That we may walk fittingly where birds sing,
That we may walk fittingly where grass is green,
Oh our Mother the Earth, oh our Father the Sky!

From SONGS OF THE TEWA
translated by Dr. Herbert Joseph Spinden

FATHER SKY (From a Navaho sandpainting)

ZUNI RITUAL POETRY

My Divine Father's life-giving breath,
His breath of old age,
His breath of waters,
His breath of seeds,
His breath of riches,
His breath of fecundity,
His breath of power,
His breath of strong spirit,
His breath of all good fortune whatsoever.
Asking for his breath,
And into my warm body
Drawing his breath,
I add to your breath now.
Let no one despise the breath of his fathers,
But into your bodies,
Draw their breath,
That yonder to where the road of our sun father comes out,
Your raods may reach;
That clasping hands,
Holding one another fast,
You may finish your roads.
To this end, I add to your breath now.
Verily, so long as we enjoy the light of day,
May we wish one another well,
Verily may we pray for one another.
To this end, my fathers,

My mothers,
My children:
May you be blessed with light;
May your roads be fulfilled:
May you grow old;
May you be blessed in the chase;
To where the life-giving road of your sun father comes out
May your roads reach;
May your roads all be fulfilled.

From SAYATACA'S NIGHT CHANT
translated by Ruth Bunzel

A ZUNI PRAYER

From wherever my children have built their shelters,
May their roads come in safety.
May the forests
And the brush
Stretch out their water-filled arms
And shield their hearts;
May their roads come in safety,
May their roads be fulfilled.

From ZUNI RELIGIOUS LIFE
translated by Ruth Bunzel

TO MOTHER EARTH

Behold! Our Mother Earth is lying here.
Behold! She giveth of her fruitfulness.
Truly, her power she gives us.
Give thanks to Mother Earth who lieth here.

Behold on Mother Earth the growing fields!
Behold the promise of her fruitfulness!
Truly, her power she gives us.
Our thanks to Mother Earth who lieth here!

Behold on Mother Earth the spreading trees!
Behold the promise of her fruitfulness!
Truly her power she gives us.
Give thanks to Mother Earth who lieth here.

Behold on Mother Earth the running streams!
Behold the promise of her fruitfulness!
Truly her power she gives us.
Give thanks to Mother Earth who lieth here.

From THE HAKO, A PAWNEE CEREMONY
translated by Alice Fletcher

MOTHER EARTH (From a Navaho sandpainting)

NIGHT CHANT OF THE CA'LAKO

When in the spring,
Your earth mother is wet,
In your earth mother
You will bury these seeds,
Carefully they will bring forth their young.
Bringing them back,
Toward this your thoughts will bend.
And henceforth, as kindred,
Talking kindly to one another,
We shall always live.
And now indeed it has come to pass.
His seeds,
His riches,
His power,
His strong spirit,
All his good fortune whatsoever,
We shall give to you
To the end, my children, my fathers,
So long as we enjoy the light of day,
We shall greet one another as kindred,
Verily, we shall pray that our raods may be fulfilled.

From the Night Chant of Hekapa'kwe Ca'lako
ZUNI RITUAL POETRY
translated by Ruth Bunzel

BREATH OF LIFE

We are grateful,
*   O Mother Earth*
For the mountains
*   And the streams*
Where the deer, by
*   command of thy*
Breath of life, wander.

Wishing for you the
*   Fullness of life,*
We shall go forth prayerfully
*   upon the trails of our*
Earth Mother.

From ZUNI FETISHES
by Frank Hamilton Cushing

DEER

NAVAHO HOUSE BLESSING CEREMONY

May it be delightful, my house;
From my head to my feet, may it be delightful;
Where I lie, all above me,
All around me, may it be delightful.

May it be delightful, this gift from
Sun (day carrier), my mother's ancestor,
May it be delightful as I walk around my house;
May it be delightful, this road of light,
        my mother's ancestor.

May it be delightful, my fire;
May it be delightful for my children;
May all be well;
May it be delightful with my food and theirs;
May all my possessions be well, and may they be made
        to increase;
All my flocks, well may they be made to increase.

translated by Victor Mindileff

SLEEPY BIRD LULLABY

There are many sleepy little birds,
Sleepy little birds, sleepy little birds.
So go to sleep, my little girl,
My little Frosted-Cockle-Burr,
O, come you sleepy little birds
And slumber on her hollow eyes
That she may sleep the livelong day,
That she may sleep the livelong night.

From SONGS OF THE TEWA
translated by Dr. Herbert Joseph Spinden

SAN JUAN RAIN SONG

Ready we stand in San Juan town,
Our Corn Maidens and Corn Youths!
Our Corn Mother and Corn Father!
Now we bring you misty water
And throw it different ways,
To the north, the west, the south, the east,
To heaven above and the drinking earth below!
Then likewise throw your misty water
Toward San Juan!
Many that you are, pour water
All around about us here
On Green Earth Woman's back.
Now thrive our flesh and breath,
Now grows our strength of arm and leg,
Now take form our children's food!

From PUEBLO INDIAN RELIGION
by Elsie Clews Parsons

SEED-THINGS

Watch well o'er your seed-things and children!
Speak wisely to these our new children!
Henceforth they shall be your first speakers,
And the peace-making shields of your people.

ZUNI CREATION MYTH
translated by Frank Hamilton Cushing

BLUEBIRD ON CLOUDS AND SUNFLOWER PLANT

A LETTER OF THANKS

*Father, through your will we are
this day happy, when, but for your
will we had been heavy with thoughts.
Thank you, our father.*

*May the sun of all summers that number
your years find you as happy as were your
Zuni children when they listened to the
words of you and your chiefs—words which
sounded to their ears and to their hearts
as beautiful as to the eyes look a vale
of flowers.*

*A letter of thanks to President Chester A.
Arthur for the return of Nutria Springs and
many acres of land being taken from the Zuni
Indians by some unscrupulous white men.*

SUN AND BLUEBIRD ON FLOWERS

RAINBOW, SUN, CLOUDS, PLANTS

A PRAYER FOR HEALING

You who dwell in the house of dawn,
In the house made of the evening twilight,
In the house made of dark mist,
Where the zigzag lightning stands high on top,
Oh, male divinity! Come to us, come.

With the zigzag lighning flung over your head,
      come to us soaring!
With the rainbow hanging high on the ends of your wings,
      come to us soaring!
I have made the right offering;
I have prepared a smoke for you.

My feet restore for me,
My legs restore for me,
My body restore for me,
My mind restore for me,
My voice restore for me,
Today take away your spell from me.
Far off you have taken it.
Happily I recover.

With beauty before me, I walk,
With beauty behind me, I walk,
With beauty below me, I walk,
With beauty above me, I walk,
With beauty all around me, I walk,
In beauty it is finished.

From THE NAVAHO NIGHT CHANT
translated by Dr. Washington Matthews

THE ORIGIN OF CORN

It is well, brothers younger!
Dwell in peace by our firesides.
Guard the seed of our maidens
Each kind as ye see it,
Apart from the others,
And by lovingly toiling,
As by toiling and loving,
Men win the full favor
And hearts of their maidens.
So, from year unto year
Shall ye win by your watching,
And power of beseeching,
And care for the corn-flesh,
The favor and plenish
Of our seven Corn Maidens.
They shall dance for the increase
And strength of the corn-seed,
Of each grain, making many,
Each grain that ye nourish
With new soil and water!

From ZUNI CREATION MYTH
translated by Frank Hamilton Cushing

CORN MAIDEN

TO MOTHER CORN

See! The Mother Corn comes hither,
Making all hearts glad!
Give her thanks, she brings a blessing.
Now, behold! she is here!
Yonder Mother Corn is coming,
Coming unto us!
Peace and plenty she is bringing;
Now behold! She is here!

From THE HAKO, A PAWNEE CEREMONY
translated by Alice Fletcher

THANKS FOR GIFTS FROM MOTHER CORN

Rev'rent our hearts turn unto the
One who brings to us
Long life and children, peace,
And the gifts of strength and food.
Rev'rent our hearts turn unto our Mother Corn!

Rev'rent our hearts turn unto the
Source whence come to us
Long life and children, peace,
And the gifts of strength and food,
Gifts from Tira'wa, sent through our Mother Corn.

From THE HAKO, A PAWNEE CEREMONY
translated by Alice Fletcher

OH, EAGLE, COME!

Oh, Eagle, come, with wings outspread
in sunny skies!
Oh, Eagle, come, and bring us peace,
thy gentle peace!
Oh, Eagle, come, and give new life
to us who pray!

From THE HAKO, A PAWNEE CEREMONY
translated by Alice Fletcher

EAGLE

A PRAYER FOR ALL PEOPLE

May all tame animals increase and children all,
For little people are we all to be loved of the Gods
As far away as our Great Mother's sound of breathing
Reaches. Even to the Utes, Apaches, Navahos, Kiowas,
Comanches, Cheyennes, even to all of them!
To the Mexican people, even to them it reaches!
To the people of America, even to them the sound
Of our Great Mother's breathing reaches.

So now they are loved of the Gods and each by the other loved!
So that is why we hope to find our living here,
We mortal men! Then place good summers and
Good days and nights of harvest! For each the same,
Place then good days and nights of harvest!

From SONGS OF THE TEWA
by Dr. Herbert Joseph Spinden

BIRDS, DEER, PLANTS

LOOK UP MY CHILD

Look! my child, who is coming unto you;
Look up, my little one, now your trouble
Goes away, away;
Look! Above you flies one who guards you,
Whose presence brings you joy.
Now your sorrow has departed.

Ah, you look!
See the eagles flying over you,
From up above they come,
From the clear blue sky where Father dwells;
They to you this peace-bringing solace give.
A happy little child now is smiling here,
Light-hearted.

From Incidental Rituals, THE HAKO
translated by Alice Fletcher

WORKS CONSULTED

Bunzel, Ruth. *Zuni Ritual Poetry.* Bureau of American Ethnology Report No. 47, 1929-1930.

Cushing, Frank Hamilton. *Zuni Breadstuff.* Indian Notes and Monographs, Vol. VIII. Museum of the American Indian, Heye Foundation, New York City, 1920.

Cushing, Frank Hamilton. *Zuni Fetishes.* Bureau of American Ethnology Report No. 2, 1880-1881.

Fletcher, Alice. *The Hako, A Pawnee Ceremony.* Bureau of American Ethnology Report No. 22, Part 2, 1900-1901.

Matthews, Dr. Washington. *The Mountain Chant, Navaho.* Bureau of American Ethnology Report No. 5, 1883-1884.

Matthews, Dr. Washington. *The Navaho Night Chant.* American Museum of Natural History. Memoirs, Vol. VI, 1913.

Mindileff, Victor. *House Blessing, Navaho.* Bureau of American Ethnology Report No. 17, 1895-1896.

Parsons, Elsie Clews. *Pueblo Indian Religion.* Vol. 1, University of Chicago, 1939.

Spinden, Dr. Herbert Joseph. *Songs Of The Tewa.* The Exposition of Indian Tribal Arts, Inc. New York, 1933.